Michael Vince

Long Distance

Long Distance published in the United Kingdom in 2020

by Mica Press

47 Belle Vue Road, Wivenhoe, Colchester, Essex CO7 9LD
www.micapress.co.uk | books@micapress.co.uk

ISBN 978-1-869848-25-5

Copyright © 2020 Michael Vince

The right of Michael Vince to be identified as the author of this work has been asserted by him in accordance with the Copyright, Designs and Patents Act of 1988.
All rights reserved.

Cover:
Blue House on the Shore, c.1930-1, Paul Nash, Tate. Photo © Tate
Detail from 'Over London by Rail', 1872, Gustav Doré.
Photo © Museum of London

Some of these poems have appeared in the following publications:
Numbers, Verse, Gaining Definition, A Few Friends

Contents

CAMBERWELL

CAMBERWELL	1
MUSIC HALL	2
ELEANOR COADE	3
THE LAVA RINK	4
CHARLIE AND ME	5
A CAMBERWELL WEDDING	6
FREE HOUSE	7
THE BARD OF THE GROVE	8
LAST GATE POST	9
JOHN COAKLEY LETTSOM: FAMILY PORTRAIT	10
LETTSOM'S VILLA	11
LETTSOM FOUND	12
DOG KENNEL HILL	14
MR AND MRS RUSKIN AND JOHN	15
THE WALWORTH JUMPERS	16
STRETCHERS	17
CAMBERWELL FAIR	18
PERSONS DISTRACTED	21
PREFAB	22
ST GILES, CAMBERWELL	23
URBAN BEES	24

LONG DISTANCE

WAKING	28
BODYSWERVE	29
BUILT IN A DAY	30
THE RETURN OF PENELOPE	31
BEING ALONE	32
NATURE MORTE	33
DIARY	34
GODDESS	35
THE CROSSES	36
TEMPLE OF APHRODITE	37

FAMILIAR LAND	38
LONG DISTANCE	39
HOUSE ON THE SHORE – a variation	40
A VOYAGE TO KYTHERA	41

BOOKLAND

BOOKLAND	44
ELTHAM	45
THE RAILWAY CARRIAGES	48
FIGUREHEAD	50
AN OLD STORY	51
GREAT GOOD HOUSE	52
OLD MAN	53
THE SWORD	54
PATCHES OF PATTERNING	57
SILENT POOL	58
STONE TURTLE	59
TIME BACKWARDS	60

THE ORDINARY

ELY APHRODITE	62
THE ORDINARY	63
GOAT LAND	64
JASMINE	65
FLIP SIDE	66
BROADCAST	67
SUMMER	68

CAMBERWELL

CAMBERWELL

A brief overture

A dreadlocked boy on an undersized bike weaves among cars.
The abandoned trudge back and forth past the bus-stops.
Past dwellers rise, not understood, and descend finally.

*'The dance ceremony takes its twisting mystical journey
where the movement accelerates the abandonment of self,
and those who attain truth arrive at some perfection.'*

Dervish turns of direction make new paths in historical
fragments, not round in harmony, but pushed apart:
discarded selves, empty visions, beliefs left on shelves.

As Mister Blake of Lambeth once walking these lost fields.
As old rooms and gardens, furnished with inexact *phaenomena*.
As the Fair. The Music Hall gas flare. The polished Lava floor.

Hidden by terrace and high-rise the late sun catches
the blade of the Tower at Elephant, evening's brief word,
its pillar of desert fire, its flaming paradisiacal sword.....

MUSIC HALL

Come and have a look at what I've got.
This slant view from a cracked pane
to a grimed house-back,
the stump of a shoulder pallid in the cold
room, smoke warm for a second as a plume of breath.

Every body works but Father.
I sit at the hearth all day. Work I say
is like the street, pitted cobbles, pooled horse-piss.
A hot man who falls against you, turns, and spits.

And the parrot says, 'I don't think'.
I've asked them many times to give me a chance,
or just the once to tell the truth.
There is shouting, music is playing,
I think I might. But I don't.

It isn't the girl I saw you with at Brighton.
So sing again and drink up and so on.
It's the warmth of a spree, Saturday night.
Clothes on the chair and don't turn on the gas.

I always hold with having it if you fancy it
but it's out of reach, houses get in the way.
The slum entry, the dust heap, that's me,
Night sky's stage, eternal lamps unlit.

ELEANOR COADE

Coade Stone

Camberwell Grove 1821

Stony in an airless room in a Georgian
terrace of lodgings, the old woman slackens
into death, body and mind hard around
the end of things. Outside the world it seems
has been moulded into stone, factitious
conglomerate of passing birds, and curling clouds.
The cast-men cry as they measure fragments,
radiance of neighbouring window-glass,
then clays and flint powdered into the mix.
Twice fired under furnace heat, three times
inspired with living power, a newborn
rubs at its clammy eyes with orange fists,
a shape renewed alive from the catalogue,
old siren, goddess, weather-proof motif.

THE LAVA RINK

Grove Lane, Camberwell Grove

Just down the road, on an empty space
above the railway tunnel, between
two blocks of flats, grassed over now,
was the square metal-framed
shed of the Lava Rink. On this postcard
its inside walls have distant
mountain views, lights hang from the roof's
metal trusses, but no sign of skaters,
circling, turning (thanks to
Mr Plimpton's patent skates)
sweeping round to music perhaps,
holding hands, laughing and falling.

The name gives it away:
no sweep of blades,
no muffled girls with gloves and scarves,
for here no ice, but fire
impressed from memory in the floor
rules over the proceedings.

Crushed polished stone, was it
really imported from Vesuvius,
or was that a promotional boast?
It must have made the skaters shudder
that image of the fiery pit,
as they wheeled round and round,
erupting molten rock
rolling from the sides towards towns
far below –
while under them in the tunnel,
steam engines roared and spewed
smoke and fine ash.
                    The rink
burned to the ground a century ago,
the company that ran it
having lost money closed it down,
the lava floor, no longer
polished by happy roller-skaters,
has become a buried thought fading
past the flats, down the Grove,
one more cold stain warming into memory.

CHARLIE AND ME

North Kent and Camberwell

Digging out footings in the cold fifty years ago:
'Just a slice of turf, then gravel, and it's pug under.'
What was it? I couldn't ask, he was rather deaf,
my mother's cousin. He rushed suddenly at work:
his brothers and his working men called him Blunder.
So we stared at the trench then got to grips with the stuff.
He leaned hard into it and showed me how.

As the day hangs frosted in memory, that slabbed clay
sticks to my spade. Clay meant brickfields: centuries
of barges brought down London waste and spoil
and took back Swale yellows. They pumped life blood
from the wharf at Deptford along canal arteries
to Camberwell Cut or Peckham Eagle, sheer toil
building up arched miles of Victorian railway:

my imaginary photo shows the deep work space
where hatted men in tied trousers, dusty boots
and waistcoats, line this cutting with walls of yellow,
laying hundreds of bricks a day for a few bob.
A bowler-hatted foreman in top-coat and suit
completes the pose. If only each brick might show
the man's name who mortared it into place

incised, not like today's tags, KORN or DED,
sprayed-on pride or anger. Their work might cling
here as the spade's surface was gripped then
one day in the cold: brickmakers, bricklayers,
held a second by the lens opening and closing,
fired to hardness like bricks, those dissolved men,
bound deep by walls yet unheld and unlimited.

A CAMBERWELL WEDDING

Great Expectations

The world of deception from which money and power come,
which governs how people are named, housed, fed, employed,
and the world where the boy hero grew up, a confusion of earth,
standing water, river mist, the blank staring of cattle,

where wealth that makes the gentleman proceeds from crime
it seems, and hundreds must stand silent in courtroom judgement
to be sent Away, or be hanged - these two worlds are one.
Here the delusions of the Child are unsettlingly many,

for this is fiction and the author is entangled in the pretence
that One may be innocent, beloved, requiring warm protection,
yet his Wife kept from knowledge must not find out:
he steers things his way, with occasional shafts of hope

slanting like sunlight through river haze. So one morning
along the Walworth Road come this paper-thin couple,
he a minor character, secretly devoted Son
of an Aged Father, and she an invisible comic turn

always unclasping smartly his flat encroaching hand.
Over his shoulder as distraction he carries a fishing-rod:
no, just out for a stroll. But quietly in St Giles,
the Aged, after missing his cue and getting a prompt,

gives Miss Steffens away to Mr Wemmick with Pip
as best man, witness, and authorial representative
of illusion. The party walks on past Camberwell Green
and up to the distant rising ground for the wedding breakfast,

at the corner of Champion Hill, perhaps, the road Ruskin
advised his visitors wryly not to mistake for his own.
The Bride, explains Wemmick, has a wonderful way with fowl.
The places we know still exist, even though the people

invented to live in them, we know do not. Perhaps
they partake of a real presence, for what we witness here
is illusory human conjoining of lines written on the map
with delusive earth and absence smothered deep below it.

FREE HOUSE

A gale outside, snow flying before, in the snug
out of the way a fuddled constable, a blaze
of good fellowship and fire and song and smoke
in the parlour, none of which could ever end.
What is your best – your very best – ale a glass?

Outside the damp jakes in the cobbled yard
a stink worse than the shambles of horse stale,
exhaustion, disenfranchisement, bitter coinage
and some activities which you wouldn't call
respectable against the wall by the back gate

*Just draw me a glass of the Genuine Stunning
if you please.* Beside this fiction propping the bar
stand figures scuffing the sawdust, men smoking
by the open fire, the six in the corner playing
queen in the hole with the greasy pack of cards,

and a few half mouthing a song and a couple of girls
no better than they should be in a dance together,
where the *Golden Lion* shines more bright indeed
than the *Midday Sun* with its cheery grin, and where
The Tiger does not indeed with *The Lamb* lie down

as the roadmen never get on well with the boys
from the pickle factory. Children call jug in hand,
beer for father. Cockles are for sale outside
as streets empty, houses start tumbling about,
a fog swirls from doors then drips into morning,

drifts off with all in its grasp – and butt and tun,
gaslights, wooden settles, sink and fade,
the *Barley Mow* cut down, and dear *Prince Albert*
under his slab as the *Swan* on its final song
falls and exhales the pent yard's sooted breath.

THE BARD OF THE GROVE

Unknown writer, Camberwell Grove

Faint birdsong, slant light on leafless boughs,
smoke from kitchen fires hazes dawn air.
Footsteps of servants, outside whisperings
scuff of feet, creaking of hay carts,
muffled slam of doors and the wind's noise.

In bed and I won't stir. Frost stars the glass,
my suit of clothes hollow and damp in a corner,
empty when I should rise wash and dress
and haste to Mr Dodd's to tend the green shoots
wilting there in his Academic Wilderness.

Warmed after wine last night, book on knee
I wrote to the light of an oozing candle stub,
versing and crossing, inching word after word,
but pulled up short, thrown by the Wingèd Steed,
muddily back down to earth, unable to Fly.

Then with my verses I built a funeral pyre
in the fire's last embers, and blew until they flared
and floated up the chimney as blackened leaves.
Outside a fox sang out, away up the hill,
an echoing sound sharp across the cold air.

Mr Browning lived at home until his mid thirties.
Mr Hood who once praised the air of Camberwell
dwelt by the Green, hoping not to disconcert
his nerves. This place does not favour a Muse
perhaps, doe-faced and garlanded with civilities,

but needs one straight eyed, robust as a beam of iron,
keeping its house where flowers carved into wood
give way to foul-stained brick, sour-smelling drains,
a tenant made of stone thrice tempered in fire
not a blinded bird singing in a cage on its own.

LAST GATE POST

One pillared gate post with the name of a house
blurred by years of rain, the family mansion
its lawns and stately elms uprooted, abraded

back to the level then measured, pegged out,
dug out, built over, the surviving invisible
empty gate through which a past place shows

its outline, its faded structure the mockery
of a living creature uncovered by explorers
on a hostile world. *We can make it live and grow*

someone declares, and in sealed conditions
its habitat is reborn: misty days, damp leaves,
a hansom cab's creak and clop, the washerwoman

with raw hands closing the basement door,
two coal heavers delivering hundredweights,
Master with his cane, his cigar, his long overcoat

and Mistress in a ball dress coming home late.
There is a light in the hall. Servants have waited up.
Unfortunate incidents, those deaths, air-raids,

unwind as a chain of events, curl like a railway
where wagons laden with heaps of the past
retrieved in detail shudder finally to a halt

with a screech of brakes at the fall of a signal arm,
a chopping blade. It slices away years
to leave this single post pared to its blank

upright story, its carved singular name.

JOHN COAKLEY LETTSOM: FAMILY PORTRAIT

after Zoffany perhaps

In this painting you hold the hand of your little son,
touching the elder's shoulder: the tiny one holds a telescope,
the elder, nine or ten, has boots on just like yours.

By the wall with its inevitable decorative classical urn
sits your wife: your daughter beside her nurses a rabbit
which is stroked by a small girl; another girl or boy

is petting the family dog. You all bear grave expressions
for you are serious folk, free, and close to God,
industrious and rich, a considerable success story

of eighteenth century London. You come from far away
Tortola, tiny turtle dove, one of the Virgin islands,
an island with a Lettsom School, but not named after you,

and even an airport which carries the family name. Here
great jets aim at Elephant Tower and thrust and turn
above your overbuilt garden and your archaeological villa,

bringing perhaps the surges of Caribbean and Atlantic
to shake the invisible branches of your well-chosen trees,
the ideas that you planted, and worked to root and grow.

LETTSOM'S VILLA

Slave trade winds rustle in the palm-tree fronds
And potted tea bushes and hardwood trees
Where on its hill this tract of rational London
Shows off well-ordered Roman certainties.

After your round of visits, here you spend
Your leisure hours, doctor of many parts,
The loving father, the hospitable Friend,
The gardener and curator of the arts.

Here Boswell once drank rather too much wine,
And other guests flowed in occasional verse.
How smile the statues in your garden shrine!
How sweet your shaded walks, how deep your purse!

You dined with Johnson once, but held your tongue
And let the old man talk. What Johnson said
Of Dr Levet would be slightly wrong:
Not quite 'the friend of friendless men', instead

You moved among the Friends, and made your way.
Order you loved, and curiosities,
Well-catalogued and labelled for display,
Sea-shells and rocks, doubtful antiquities.

Yet far-away Tortola kept your soul,
A separate simpler world, born of hard toil,
Mainly the work of slaves: you were 'creole'
You always said, a native of that soil.

Those slaves who raised you, they were family
Whose love still held you when you were apart.
So when you came of age you set them free,
But never cast them loose out of your heart.

Your vista long built over, still the slow
Course of the Peck winds under, hidden where
Your garden ghosts the hillside with its flow,
And breaths of your lost trees enrich the air.

LETTSOM FOUND

1 A Sketch of Dr Lettsom

Founder of the Medical Society,
Founder of the General Dispensary.

Founder of the Seabathing Hospital
Margate, for the Poor of London.

Author of Diseases of Great Towns,
And the Best Means of Preventing them,

Of Hints on Medical Education,
The Natural History of the Tea Tree

And of many other pamphlets
Including An Account of the Culture

And Use of the Mangel Wurzel,
Also called The Root of Scarcity.

Promoter of Inoculation.
Collector of Curiosities.

You and your brother the only survivors
Of seven sets of male twins.

2 From the Sale of Dr Lettsom's Possessions

A print of Margate viewed from the Parade.
A large and fine horn of a unicorn.
Two very powerful magnets. Many coins.
A seal of Benjamin Franklin carved in wood.

Part of the bottom of Lord Anson's ship
Called *The Centurion*. Butterflies and moths.
Patterns for Farthings from the Commonwealth.
A very Curious Canadian Pipe.

A Nautilus fossil from the *Archway* chalk.
Mosaic Pavement in a Mahogany case,
From *Leadenhall Street*. Pressed specimens of Grass.
Otaheite Cordage and Fish Hooks.

An Indian Fan made of the Palm Leaf,
A Fine Cylindrical Mirror made of Steel.
A model Guillotine, a Metal Seal,
A Mummy from the Isle of Teneriffe.

A Wooden Box of Chinese Butterflies.
An Electrical Machine with Thunder House.
A Scalping Knife. A Fly Flap. Snow shoes.
Some Emblematical Transparencies.

A Pair of Curious Bronze Candlesticks,
Flies' Nests and Wasps' Nests, Arrows, Clubs and Spears.
A quantity of Minerals in drawers.
A set of Chessmen in a Chinese Box.

DOG KENNEL HILL

Market gardens covered this place
between railway and hill brow
until the builders pegged out plots
more than a hundred years ago:

it was rough pasture or downland
before lines of beans and lettuce.
There was water. People lived here:
voices and faces are shapeless

and cannot argue for ownership
or who came first. They are known
by no name or written form,
all their lives overgrown

like land and what lies under it,
below thought, beneath notice,
out of time, ghosts. Our cats
stare at nothing, unknown plants

appear in the garden, floorboards
creak though no-one steps on them,
brief unintelligible words,
shapes tracing a diagram.

We will reach that horizon
where lines converge, disappear,
in time just undergrowth
on a hill, below miles of air.

MR AND MRS RUSKIN AND JOHN

The creaking of that vast custom-built wooden vehicle,
the nineteenth century, along the leagues of pavé measured
by low sunlight flickering through the regular sentinel poplars.
Inside there are cubby-holes and deep pockets for everything,
a shelf of books, a writing desk, necessary medicines and a commode,
cold cutlets, soda water, a whole ham, and a selection of wines.

Mother requires the learning by heart and reciting of a bible chapter.
From time to time at a convenient stop John is allowed to play
unsupervised, or with well-chosen young people of the locality.
Products of iron such as false pillars, railways, hand-made nails,
or the Crystal Palace, rust slightly under blasts of John's anathema,
cursèd things, to be contrasted, in the same word, with devoted things,

the things he loves: rock specimens, structures of leaf and flower,
products of artistic worship and patience. These all rattle around
as the travelling diligence, if that's what it is, rolls ever onwards
towards the Alps. Father looks on at his son, and is pleased,
for the wine business has prospered, and there's money for good hotels,
for the best and latest Turners, for the subsidising of writing,

and employment of suitable servants and the taking of house and grounds
in the cleaner air of Camberwell. And the wheels lumber on
through a whiff of factory chemicals, the fiery pouring out of steel,
the beautiful fluted barrel of the Maxim gun, the gathering future
falling from air as soot, as the Passenger Pigeon, as the distant glint
of sunlight on places where snow once lay carpeted in silence.

THE WALWORTH JUMPERS

> *'Leave the world's ways, and give up all earthly and carnal usages, and live for me'*
>
> Mary Ann Girling

> *'My experiences beneath the railway arch at Walworth are only the latest, and certainly not the most picturesque or interesting, edition of phenomena rather curious than uncommon.'*
>
> Rev. C M Davies Unorthodox London 1876

The saints crowd into the place with its arched roof,
the walls rough patched with damp. Thunder overhead
of passing trains, taunts of local youths, windows
reflecting weak gas jets: the Reverend Davies sits
by the 'carpenter's table' at the front and watches
the brothers and sisters exchange kisses of welcome,

much to the derision of the 'New Cut swells'
who have pushed their way in past the feeble
representative of security. Will they dance tonight
and leap about, the faithful, and are they under
hypnotic influence, 'animal magnetism', the staring eye
of the 'minister' in her red gown and black bonnet?

They pray, they sing, the minster preaches a sermon.
They are much concerned with the afterlife, with death
and the absence of death, with the eternity they now have,
since they have died already and been cleansed of all sin
and started afresh. Another train rumbles overhead,
some little girls and a 'hobbledehoy' begin to dance,

that is all. In the wooded scrub of the New Forest,
their spiritual home awaits. All goods in common,
no personal possessions, no marriage, no carnality:
all shall till the fields, no produce shall be sold,
as time gives a jump or two and imitates Eden
or St George's Hill Weybridge, the Diggers' common land

worked for the Lord. There will be only rainbows
not railway arches, only steam from soaked bushes
in summer heat after a squall, not the black finger
of boiler smoke, driven by coal scraped from Hell
by men, women, children. There we shall dance indeed,
leap clear of the fallen world to be lodged in Paradise.

STRETCHERS

hospital stretchers, Dog Kennel Hill

Metal stretchers, stacked up ready
for victims and along the hill
still top this brick wall edging
the estate, their rusted wire
mesh and metal pole supports

Recruits march in their photograph
along East Dulwich Road
while engines shunt hospital carriages
up a vanished siding by the station:
wounded men carried gently
on stretchers into the wards

Grief to end all Grief
the abundant dead, generations
of black-clad women, the fatherless,
the friendless, their parades
fewer each year, this memorial
ghosting of stretchers on walls
lifted finally and carried away

Stretchers built into helmeted men,
mouths meshed against gas,
torn metal limbs, dull cast uniforms,
the litter bin by the bus-stop now
a head its gas-mask welded on:
their memorial that helmet face

dead and wounded men the shape
gently on stretchers down the hill

CAMBERWELL FAIR

1 Puppet Play

Cool yourself in the shade, you and your gawping friends.
See, the Infernal King conveys the lop-sided effigy
of the Pope into the fire, and there knavery mounts
its gingerbread hobbyhorse. And so to the old man
dancing upon the ropes despite his many falls,
with a duck on his head and with a wheelbarrow before him
with two dirty children and a dog in it. The old man sings
and everyone laughs at the bears dancing like ladies
and admires the lions, tigers, panthers, hyenas, ostriches,
pelicans and storks. But the ballad he sings tells of love,
not of the drabs lurking in darkness nor of the beauty
who cuts her meat with a knife between her toes, but rather
the tale of his abandoned daughter. *All, all is lost,*
my life has been cast down, I weep and cannot stir,
for I am the abandoned love of the handsome Puppet Player
who has cut the strings of my heart and I cannot leave the Fair.

2 Sleight of hand

And the curtains parted and I stood on tiptoe as much
as I could, and the Mermaid combed her hair, a wig
for certain, and the tip of her tail poked out
above the water, if that's what it was, and the lads
behind me pressed me close and I turned to have words
and little Amelia grizzled and screwed up her pink face
but I sent them packing, the nerve of it, that's the trouble
with Fairs, constable, and I arranged her new bonnet
and that's when there was a faint tug, and I felt around
for the money I'd buttoned into my coat and the very cloth
was slit all through, so gentle that I'd hardly felt it,
and whether it was those two or another in the crowd
who can tell, for the Mermaid I thought gave me a wave
and her face shined in a smile as if there was magic in it.

3 Before the end

1826 The child John Ruskin

The moving fair was under his feet he could feel it rocking
gently as if he sat on the river ferry with the water flowing
and along there on the vanished ground the small boy watched
his sailing boat tip in the wind on a long ago filled in pond,
a lost child so anxious to see The Fair that he stopped too long
to watch the Performing Pig and everyone else had walked on
called by the whistle and bell announcing the puppet show
so that when he had stared long at the Pig, which was stubbornly
not Performing, there was no hand to hold and he couldn't see
through the forest of legs, and *Bow Wow What a Row*
but unburdened with tears or even the slightest fear, he climbed
onto the stage where the Conjuror stood uttering the magic
lost words, and the Fair was rebuilt in brick, stone and glass
and everyone danced into this Cathedral and shouted Amen.

PERSONS DISTRACTED

The voice was given to me, but I was not master of it

John Perceval

Some seek a refuge as at 'Bethlehem' to soothe the mind
Where holy fields may glow green with palm fronds
Or with golden crowns woven from rising grain.
So leave her in the dark, bind him with fiery chains:

These are the self-deceived broken by their imaginings,
Worshippers who believe they are in hell and that brick steps
Edging the foul abyss that floats with smoke and roars out
Lead them to punishment, not to the marsh-ground gaslight

Of railway platforms. It is another journey they are on,
A departure of speech turning round and staying within
The sheltering walls of these locked-up lodging places,
Pacing and repeating, the trapped, the repressed forces

Of springs built over and channelled away beneath streets.
Outside horses pass, figures in long coats raise hats,
A man walks home carrying two rabbits in a poke.
These ones inside may be hung like game in the dark,

Until they are tender enough and may be cut down,
Stripped of feathers and fur and jarred to the bone,
Hollow, silent, drained clean of all mother and father
As carts around the Green rumble on hither and thither.

PREFAB

East Dulwich

The explosion among the houses is a message from far off
distributing pains of slavery, sounds of suffering, beaten
life given instructions sharpened into orders based upon
a cult of efficiency hidden beneath a mountain of hard
ineptitude. The noise of destruction comes after a brief
rush of silence, when the pulse of the engine, its mounting
at the rear of the projectile, like a handle, stops, and as
if the giant hand of an angry child beat the thing downwards.
Later in the space cleared by this violence built upon death
houses are put up, simple prefabs, temporary homes.

One afternoon we stop and chat with the man digging his garden
some seventy years later. Well tended dahlias and chrysanths,
cabbages in rows, a garden frame, everything except a Pig:
this is the small-holder's dream, the exemplary cottage garden,
a prefabricated world. Kids growing up, boys in long socks
with catapults, mock the weapon on its thrusting ramp;
labourers trapped in tunnels, dead of disease or starved,
rise in the memorial of children at play among the willow-herb.
Rockets rise at Guy Fawkes from gardens with gasps of joy,
erasing the smoke script of hatred from a strip of dirty sky.

ST GILES, CAMBERWELL

Leave off all advantage of birth,
garments of silk with gold threads:
quit your loving parents, abandon
wealth, possessions, and head forth
down dusty unsigned roads
to where nobody has gone.

Alone in the green wood
eat only the forest plants
or food brought by those who come
searching after sainthood,
blessing, wisdom, reassurance,
if only you can help them.

Avoid the intrusive hunt.
Accept the spear wound, the arrow
in defence of the blameless deer
and build on that sacrifice or its variant
until of great age, your body a shadow,
you take boat to a far shore.

In a nearby cave put away
your flesh and await release
so that you may become a wise
minor god with a name day,
your attributes in altar piece
and stained glass. Specialise

in the hopeless sick and the homeless,
those whose limbs go awry,
the dispossessed, those in despair,
writhing like twisted forest trees,
those who are stricken with leprosy
who wake screaming out of nightmare,

all those hurt in body or mind.
Sit long cradling the distraught
deer - the arrow in its wound
passes through your comforting hand,
an illumination, a shaft of thought
piercing the dark ancient land.

URBAN BEES

Here is my poem about fields and flocks and trees

                                                  Virgil *Georgics*

for Robert Wells

Bees come to drink from a plastic pot base
green with algae, floating with dead leaves,
water our cats prefer. The bees lean down
from the lip to drink – some fall and thrash about
in the shallow water. We use a wooden spoon
to lift them out, and leave them there to dry.
Our neighbour with the hives along the road
laughs about it. *They like to drink away
when they are hard at work.* A friend complained
how thirsty bees swooped over the jacuzzi
out in his garden, how his children screamed.
At dusk the urban bees have flown for home
but for several days they visit us and drink:
word must have got around. This year, oddly,
as if at their command, a growth of clover
unseen before, has risen in the lawn.
The bees circle, and hover at its sweetness.
They forget about the water. They have moved on,
busy for better necessary things.

The neighbour's garden is planted for the bees,
neatly kept and stocked with plants they love,
pots of sage and lavender and a lilac.
This year it looks unpruned, perhaps unwatered.
The keeper's wife who planned and tended it,
walked up and down and talked to everyone
along the road, now has a wraith-like look,
a small pale ghost of water, not a gleam.
As bees come back and forth, it seems her spirit
has drained or flown, she barely speaks or eats.
Now the keeper and wife go back and forth
to hospital. Though strained, he smiles bravely.
I meet them walking along local streets,
trying to stay afloat like thirsty bees
who lean too far and drown in shallow water.

The stalls in farmers' markets are well stacked
with jars of London honey. Bees belong,
unknown to them, to postcodes, to some local
authority, once just the neighbouring fields,
on maps like prints of skin, a whorl of roads
on grubby palms of suburbs. Busily
in gardens, grassy spaces, cemeteries
and railway lands, the bees stoop down to sip
sweetness unseen and take it home to feed
their commonwealth - the Fat One at its centre,
the idle ones who hang about all day.
Bees that fall ill are driven from the hive.
The Fat One readies for her mating flight.

Uniformed schoolboys, nineteen sixty-three:
O-level Latin set book is a poem
about bee-keeping and its origins.
It's Virgil in a Welsh voice from a master
with a loud temper. *Sir, what's this about,
farming and stuff and tales of giants and heroes,
is it a myth?* The scansion rules depend,
it seems, on whether vowels are long or short.
Like trousers sir? There are a lot of rules:
*for nouns, or so it goes, which cannot be
declined, the neuter gender is assigned.*
Head down, and no eye contact, fingers crossed
hoping not to be singled out – there's just
a sound of buzzing. It is an offering
which we decline. Then *pastoral Apollo,
Aristaeus, the god of orchard trees
and cattle, notices a bee swarm rising
out of a rotting heifer* – *Tate and Lyle,
it's on the tin, sir.* What god showed us this
discovery, ancient muse? The buzzing noise
comes from touch rugby players in the yard.
It carries on without us as we glean
knowledge of sorts from dried-up autumn flowers.

Two boys in tangled strips of urban woodland
along the hedgerows harvest shiny damsons –
plums from the watered gardens of Damascus,
and blackthorn sloes, our bitter Saxon forbears
softened only by frost. On other days
they fill their bags with conkers, nibble at
beech mast, or suck the sweet from nettle flowers.
Stingers they say grow where old houses stood.

Today they rest from hunting moths or slugs,
and try their hands at gathering seeds from grass,
potatoes from allotments, bruised windfalls
from garden trees. Their freckled arms and legs
turn bloody in a brambled wilderness
heavy with blackberries. So chattering,
shouting and screaming, laughing – it's their buzz,
their version of bee messages, two friends
rubbing along together. Add thorn stabs
to hidden nettle stings or angry wasps:
these the deep wounds of memory, the tract
of land built over, last bees dulled by cold,
unbitten nails and knees no longer scabbed.

In urban London, children stay near home.
Here in the sun three foxes lie, just pups
beside the railway. One looks up and stares
as trains go by, one scratches at a flea,
one has curled up like a contented pet.
These are survivors, they feel comfortable,
play in our garden, sit beside the gate
or amble on the pavement checking bins.
Some limp or cower with untended wounds.
Bee hives high up on roofs of tower blocks
look down upon the city where they roam
taking uncertain refuge while they can.
If this were holy land, these would be gods
half seen at dusk. Our earnest offerings
might have been laid with reverence at their shrine.

LONG DISTANCE

WAKING

I wake at first light in an unfamiliar bed;
outside, a stir of hens, chirrup of birds,
the drip and pat of rain.

I dreamt of you, but what I dreamt of I forget.
Coffee; and then farewell; and now the car
goes easing through the lanes,

I feel your presence in my body still unblurred
by movement, as I peer to find the way.
Where the road drifts with cloud

I stop. A pinetree sways and gleams, a distinct sign.
Why do you still exist although I try
to let you fade without regret?

BODYSWERVE

Once or twice I
managed it, the bodyswerve
one Friday twisting
in the playground away
from hands ten or
twelve times through
for a try.
         Touch rugby,
it required bodily
deftness, a feint
in eyes and shoulder,
a ballet rhythm
of deception.

And lately
walking home past the flower-shops
near the Square, I practise
sending approaching shoppers
the wrong way –
         it leads
to glances and blushes
(often mine).

And as for the time
my body held constant
urgent course with yours,
did my eyes signal
one way, while the rest of me
went the other?
         Rather
I think, sensing now
our nakedness, a
crushing tackle,
if part of the mind deceives itself,
swerving from truth to hope and back,
the body holds to its course, it is
the body that makes the plan.

BUILT IN A DAY

Star-gazing from my window as I do
on warm nights, reading late, I think of you

studying at your table, till you sink
asleep across the books. Fatal to think,

distant to act, I tell myself, and write
to feel your arms around me, holding tight,

not letting go. I think of driving on
all night, all day, and breaking in upon

your still familiar sleep; I'd close the door
silently, as we learned to do before,

until your city would begin to take
shape in the early light, and so we'd wake.

Star-gazing with your picture and your name,
my city comes to daylight, still the same

struggle of shapes, as if built in a day,
and coffee tells me that you're far away

out of my reach, or lost. I know you're there,
but invisible, however much I stare.

THE RETURN OF PENELOPE

Who are these people and the house needs cleaning,
there are friends to telephone, gifts to arrange.
The dog runs up happily but soon it will be winter

for the music is playing not greetings but farewells.
Dear house, I have brought myself here as your guest.
As for my travels, I shall tell no-one about them

but stay myself in the songs of those far countries.
There I am the Giantess with the single angry eye,
and the muscly bow-women with the seared flat chests

will talk about me, and the Goddess who rules the Ocean
can stamp and fret and fog up the runways in vain.
My man's look and its cold waiting shall be settled,

like a ghost, by killing or burying, or in forgetting.
When desire returns it embraces the continuing dream,
the faithless servants, the stare of exhausted fields.

BEING ALONE

Being alone shakes me like a fever;
I watch old women on their balconies
struggling to shake blankets in the wind;
imagine being alone or dumb for ever
as winter lays its cold on certainties,
your body being too much on my mind.

That is much like the murmuring of the city,
not noticeable, then tangible with silence;
being with you is language left unsaid
folded with cold air in obscurity;
not be conscious of you would make sense,
seeing I dog your footsteps in my head.

I see you with your arms around a friend
or alone, smoking, with your puzzled face,
or sipping coffee in a small hotel.
I put myself beside you, I pretend
that someone else is here, and in my place
that he can smile and wave and wish us well.

NATURE MORTE

Dead leaves fall, gulls have come inland;
you assure me: most wounds simply heal,
I'll be happier in a month, in a year.
Your version becomes hard to understand.
I watch the mob of gulls flock and wheel,
they know what is coming, that it will come here

and pass, you say, as does the worst cold
which mirrors a dead lapse in experience;
a world half-mapped in snow grows on me.
Outside steady rain has taken hold
and sparse shrubs are washed into brilliance,
faces pale, glinting with jealousy.

Who should remain trusting or be generous
when the wind tugs in the shutters all night?
Both are at fault, you say, for our closeness together.
I can learn to smile sturdily as a house;
curtains are drawn, windows shut tight,
inside we sit at ease in warm weather.

DIARY

Her secret diary tells it, in the first
sentence that moves precisely from the page
out to the front, until it holds the stage
with calm long lines, in one smooth well-rehearsed

convincing movement, where all words are true.
Even the slightest gesture, these would say,
leads further from intention, more astray;
it glances from another's point of view

outwards, it offers how things seem to look
if you are him. This way she can create
his love for her, and then participate
as someone else, by writing in a book.

And if he disappoints her as a lover
she can rewrite his passion when it's over.

GODDESS

Piraeus

The olive seems to root in the stone,
the hard wood twisting down; it is her tree:
her bronze face shifts its colour as leaves turn.
See how her robes in time have grown
so frail, they might seem dry enough to burn,
such fragile metal, flaked and stained where she

lay centuries beneath the ground.
But now those swelling folds have met the light
still blurred with mud which masks her attributes,
and building-workers gather round
to gaze at her, and smoke, and scrape their boots.
The one whose spade first touched her knows it might

mean money, maybe a new dress
to soothe his wife. And so he makes his cross
to the All-Holy Virgin, and in case
this dim archaic holiness
with its blotched staring corpse's face
still holds a power of gain or loss

he gives her equal reverence.
Later he comes home drunk and beyond care
shouting a girl's name, with a bleeding hand,
then weeping and not making sense.
Unstirred, remote, his wife and mother stand
with neither blame nor pity in their stare.

THE CROSSES

Kalamata

There were some afternoons when wearing looks of warmth
she leaned over me, with a fringe grown long enough
to slant forward as her head bent, hiding her face.
My lips felt bruised and my jaws ached from kissing her.
In the gloom her dark shoulders slightly moved, and gleamed.
Beside the bed our clothes lay strewn across the floor.

That happened before the earthquake cracked our city.
The house still trembles slightly in the afternoon.
Evenings have grown cool. We drape the sheet above us
but then we shake it off. In sleep I dream I have
wrapped us both in a warming and soothing blue sheet
but it wrinkles in the dream, and cracks appear in it.

Outside on every house is a green or red cross
like a kiss put at the end of a child's letter.
Her mouth nuzzling at my cheek, she told me stories
about her doll, and the one about her rabbit
from the years before her father died. In the dusk
the rabbit savoured the freedom of the mown lawn.

So the closeness together of a just a few days quickly
becomes a story. The green cross means I can stay
and continue my life the way it was, before
the solid earth shook itself beneath the table.
If not, I dare not venture in, for what we had
might open and widen until I fell right through.

TEMPLE OF APHRODITE

Acrocorinthos – sacred prostitution

Her coupling with a stranger, hardly lust
devoted to the grasping of her own
anonymous emptiness, and barely just
the simply animal
warmth of the blood, holds to no principle;
the love of an unknown

soldier or merchant touches without grace.
His silver falls and clatters in the plate
to serve the goddess in her stony place.
Outside the sheer rock falls
where flocks are watered by the city walls,
to house and road and gate,

to the carved stones and measured ways of men.
The woman gazes out, across a sea
fading in blurs of distant mist, and then
draws water from a spring.
The goddess must be paid in everything.
Meanwhile, uncertainly,

the stranger starts for home, bearing the same
urging to be placated, on another
long road much harder than the way he came,
there being no offering there
to turn the wrath or fill the empty stare
of sister, wife, or mother.

FAMILIAR LAND

Athens

Tired from the boat, I walk the early street,
one bus-ride and I'm home. Going away,
how all felt different! Now I'm pleased to meet
home as it is and catch the start of day:

you peering from the bed-clothes just the same,
and the dog dancing, anxious for the park.
I deal my day out, it is a soothing game
after those hours of talking in the dark,

drinking, watching the waves, riding the great
body of metal swaying on through the sea
with groans and shudders. I don't start work till late,
then can't. Movement hasn't yet stopped in me,

the rhythm of ocean, a surging from inside.
The day loses its balance and I submit,
I wait until it floats out with the tide,
adrift and wasted. When it's dark I sit

reading and staring. The room echoes with noise,
but slows and settles when I try to stand.
Unmoved, unmoving, all assumes its poise
safe now with lights, the cold familiar land.

LONG DISTANCE

Octopus sleep, my waking
was beaten against a dry rock.
You left, the season changed,
and news came of the old poet
pulled under in the hardest grip
of all. Love-songs enlist weather,
but appearance traps its elegy,
this late lily spiking its sign
by the kitchen door.
      Can I
think hard to make cohere
an absence with the branching
roses that you tended
all those hot days?
      One more
lost singer prints the damp grass,
ghosting through autumn: once
he teased me for my dying fall.

Your empty place, and his, move
to the same cadence. So, love,
now we no longer walk or sleep,
let us at least think together
of voices stilled but unsilenced,
long-distance as the days shorten.

HOUSE ON THE SHORE – a variation

Montale: La Casa dei Doganieri
Paul Nash: Blue House on the Shore

You don't remember the blue house on the shore,
a stage set casting shadow, one dark window,
at the top of the beach by a line of fishing boats:
it's stayed there empty since those weeks we spent
still casting back its shape as slanting shadow
and densely packed inside with restless thoughts.

The south-west wind has beaten at its walls
and yet the paint seems fresh with perfect blue.
The smile has faded from the things you said:
there's no way back, nothing makes any sense.
You don't remember; your memory has dropped through
a crack in time just leaving one loose thread.

I hold on to one end of it and pull;
the house glows at the shore and still stands square.
Perhaps one shutter taps against the wall
or dried up seaweed crackles on the sand.
I hold one end of it, but you stay there
your breath held in the dark, without a sound.

Out there the background is an island where
in a pale sky a cloud hangs, bare and low.
Is that a sign? The small waves crash upon
the sand and stretch and sink along the beach.
You don't remember the house that I see now –
the one still with me, or the one that's gone.

A VOYAGE TO KYTHERA

against Baudelaire:
'Quelle est cette île triste et noire? C'est Cythère'

Looking down, the blue ocean lightly flecked
by the southern wind from Crete, her stone body
torn by earthquake, rock riven by deep faults,
there's the whole island, flattened out from this high up,
then as the plane slips sideways through deep
driven air, down towards land, bare peaks stand clear,
divided rocky fields and green plots laid out
rush closer, vine rows, pathways, clusters of hives.

Later from the village those curves of far hills
mimic the reclining goddess, sunning herself dry
after rising from the deep, seed blossom, sea foam,
water-borne Aphrodite. There is no merry parade
of festal lovers here, though below on the neighbouring
bay, beneath the bones of the castle, on sun beds
we stretch out together, then head slowly back
uphill: half way, a retired sea-captain has built

a comedy boat-shaped house, with propellers and funnels,
and sits outside, his wife beside him embroidering.
We climb, say hello. A watcher out for the truth
of what love might be, emblematic upon the cliffs,
sees no fierce birds tearing at flesh, only a few
crows that honk pig-like in flight; the sole sign
of torture might be the war-memorial by the plane-tree
in the square; and my one wish for strength or courage

only what's needed to plod up the hill behind you
after a day of talk, after venturing past the harbour
to feed cats outside a locked-up monastery. There
I watch you stoop, pour out water, hold out your hands,
and a happy cat leaps for delight, a simple motion
of being in love with more than being in love,
while the goddess turns in sleep on the hill and longer
shadows soothe us as we climb back home together.

BOOKLAND

BOOKLAND

Bookland, *bocland*, written charter, in the heart
this is field shape, it is plough land at footstep,
forests dense with darkness and older gods,
the shape of Alfred's land irrecoverable

hiked over in the rain with heavy word-pack,
dry bread, little to drink, paths inked words.
Later comes legend, old tales, the forgotten,
layered over with noble Victorian stuff,

statues of bearded men, last battle memorials,
significant stones. There, O Imperial Forbear,
perhaps fleet founder and cake burner and owner
of The Jewel, you live as lord, ghost fading

in reed pages, draining inscribed islands,
on thin sheep paths grooved across chalk-down,
stampings of coined faces, rubric of towns,
burghs laid out in red lines to repel armies

of heathen men. Etched out like skeleton
lines of Latin, wrapping the world in Saxon
tendrils where beasts peer, your lost kingdom
comes first on the page with A illuminated,

faintly on time's over-sanded palimpsest.

ELTHAM

Visit of Manuel Palaiologos, Byzantine Emperor, AD 1400

i Arrival

A grove of twisted trees choked with ivy.
Along the hill edge a file of swaddled horsemen.

This place has more than one tongue it is said.
Nobody understands but that is no matter.

Gifts are bestowed and received, speeches made.
Men drink at the fire, wash hands in silver bowls.

This is a small place, hemmed in by winter woods.
Not greater than our City and its walls far away.

ii Adam of Usk

Winter at Eltham, in this cold dead season,
I sit with the Greek visitors and listen.
What is more righteous, what is more profitable,
what helps us to confound the king's enemies,
according to man's law or God's law?
Should we defend The City, and its far away

puddles of rule with our men or money?
What might its priest-like Emperor give in return?
In the hall hung with boughs, the mighty blaze
casts in a poor light Him in his priest's robe
his long forked white beard, his gold glittering,
with all he says translated Greek to Latin

to French for the king's councillors and on
in me unspoken sounding of my blood's Welsh.
Gifts are given, precious monastic writings,
Holy Relics for their coins of New Rome,
bales of silk cloth. They have tried this everywhere,
in Italy and France, in Aragon, even in Denmark.

Most gracious words are exchanged. I remain silent.
I learned my lesson in King Richard's reign.
His folly, and our new Lord Henry's doubt,
equal in blood, public dismemberment,
and earthly trepidations, must be endured.
I fence round a city of words, I say nothing.

iii Yuletide

It is a long voyage from God's City of Constantinople
in the golden realm of the East to the petty princes of Italy,
and then by stages north across the desolate mountain fastness
of the Alps, across the watered plains and tangled forests

of France, to take ship again and land by the chalk cliffs
and process to the Royal Court of His Majesty King Henry,
in his little palace at Greenwich and at Christmastide to ride
here to His hunting lodge in the streams and groves of Eltham.

The Emperor, the Most High One, stands clothed only in white.
He and his men are long-haired and bearded as are his priests
muttering in the Greek tongue. He brings King Henry the jaw-
bone
of Saint Epikindinos and some teeth of Saint Aniperaspistos,

for the City, The Holy One, lies in danger, unprotected.
He has petitioned the courts of Europe for supplies of armed
men.
Enemies circle him about and the enemies of those enemies
not to mention the treachery of his friends. Green boughs hang

the hall of Eltham for the season, fires burn and songs are sung.
The Emperor and his men have turned up rather like the Magi,
The Three Wise Men, who travelled far to welcome Our Lord
at his birth in the poor stable. Their gifts, though, are a warning

that nothing will last, that nobody is safe, that even King Henry
might consider his cousin Richard who was tall fair and strong
a Christmas or two ago, but whose enemies plucked him down,
many days from God's far city all along a hard cold road.

THE RAILWAY CARRIAGES

New Forest

Before the bungalow was built,
between the wars they lived out here
in a ramshackle hut built up
around two railway carriages.
Shy deer peered through the forest trees
and watched the men unload the trailer,
and as the deer stalked off, they heard
the fading noise of saw and hammer.

The land sloped to a wall of oaks:
it took hard work with spade and hoe
before the garden beds came good,
potatoes well earthed up, bean sticks,
spread cabbage tops and rows of peas.

Kept close was their unspoken thought
that the Old Ones lived much like this,
their land and work and food their own,
their cottage daubed with dung and straw,
ship's timbers hauled up from the Hard
dowelled in the roof. This made it home
and land and varnished carriages
at rest, as if the gone train Guard
had waved his flag upon the wood,
and the slammed First and Second doors
closed round a shaded lowly space.

Past came the peasant with his cow,
and labourers set for home sang out
their harvest songs. A woman stood
with child on hip beside the gate
and called her hens or fed the pig.
So lay the dim embracing dream
they wrapped about them as they slept
cold in the carriages. Dawn birds
ran on the roof, a woodpecker
hammered its tune, or on still nights
they'd hear train-whistles ten miles off
or see the town lights as a glow
reflected faintly from the clouds,

criss-crossed by unseen pylon cables
that stretched out and hummed over them,
low lines that led across the world.

FIGUREHEADS

Cut from ships these carved figures
of helmeted Greeks or staring ladies
bare from the waist up, breasting
the relentless waves, gaze forward

at the unbeaten track, the course
of history, or merely complete
the curve of the bow. All who toiled
and skinned hands, or risked weather

and rolled aloft, and fell, believed
their workaday ark thus realised:
Bellerophon or good ship Venus,
its figurehead arrowing the way,

the sailors heroic as the armoured man
or in love with the pointing bust.
Now, late on the voyage, when crew
and passengers must do without

direction at the prow, blank faces
peer at bleached images
of fetish goddess or bearded godling
unable to calm the waters,

rise and fall with no company
of dolphins, driven on the sea-road
through digital tempests, computer doldrums,
beneath the circling fatal albatross.

AN OLD STORY

To have been a bondservant to his own hard father, which was how
he thought of it, was not even the half of it. What about his brothers
who had all the easy jobs, what about all the time he was wasting
until the old man died and the land was shared, and what about
the dried-up place, the rock-strewn fields, the thorn-scrub pastures?

To have said his piece after a few drinks and to have got the money
from his father, and to have taken his resentment along stony paths
and into his own hard future, just the sudden release of an arrow
curving into the brightness, but one which got lost among the boulders
when it fell. Still if there was an emptiness, it was his own to fill

with drinking cups of wine and dabbling in dishes of roast meat
and paying for everyone else, and sleeping with the dancing women,
until the days trickled out through his hands, water from a skin
worn thin and holed and discarded. When the money was used up,
so was he, and it was back to being a bondservant, but this time

to some harder bastard without a son. How hungry he was this time!
He rooted for scraps with the pigs he herded, as much an animal
as those wallowing in dust, and as others, humans, he had made so.
One day following the goats he made up his mind to swallow the cud
bitterness of failure, and to trudge back along the dust tracks

home. Nobody was there waiting on the walls to see him from afar,
and there was no fat young beast with throat ready to be cut
all for his sake. There was no greeting at all. That welcoming forgiveness
of his foolish rejection, that acceptance of his error, that reconciliation
were among the gobbets his aimless greed had slurped upon.

GREAT GOOD HOUSE

Horace et al

Even when imagined as the place of a caring lord
who sits to eat with his tenants and forgives their rents
in the bad season - when you, the invited guest,
having rattled over a long Jacobean road

settle in a warm corner and compose for your patron
a Horatian tribute to comfort, food, and drink,
to his lands which serve by delivering their fruits
into his hand; his maids fair to gaze upon

but chaste, his men obedient and strong, his herds
offering their flesh in a spirit of generosity
as good beasts should - still though, it's obvious
that it's not like that, the idea is only words

spoken to please. So the visitor passing here
who just drops in, waving a Heritage Trust
membership card, might suffer the third-degree
from a surly keeper, for notices make it clear

that the well-praised grounds and important architecture
are not to be viewed, the House a Private School,
or a Business Centre, or retreat for Meditation,
or the country home of an agèd rock star

who fishes the ponds for carp. The bought and sold
place has reduced itself to a couple of barely
habitable rooms. Its owner without an heir
cowers by a phutting gas fire with a portly old

cocker spaniel, *like a snail,* as someone found,
in the corner of his tremendous shell, the lord
of photographs, dead gaps among the rooftiles,
and a wealth of centuries gurgling round and round

to vanish with Nursery bath-time down the drain.
The fire that levelled the place could be seen for miles.
Time to be off. Past the lines of dead greenhouses
to the station, along the main road shiny with rain.

OLD MAN

New Forest

He watches his meaning slacken and loosen
and drain away, and sits now at the window

not looking out. Sparse fruit trees, plum
or pear or walnut, wrapped tangled in weed;

a thick hedge and a wall of giant oaks
late to lose leaf, where a deer seeks way

cautious through a gap for windfalls.
Past woven trees deceptively he sees

women weeding long rows of seedlings,
wet plodding horses, pale oxen at plough.

Deeper in the wood things hang from branches
dripping in the rain, swaying in the wind,

a hand notches an arrow onto bow,
there are dulled discarded helmets or sudden

rusted blades or broken spear shafts,
and dirt faced men who wave and beckon

or stand arms raised by dumped equipment.
Further on, past seated girls with the giggles

and feasting going on round the blaze,
there's a door perhaps, or a window open,

a signpost or a number written down
and unseen the rhythmic up and down noise

of blood still beating away at the temples,
of traffic passing and repassing along the B road....

THE SWORD

1

The blade forged by a god honed and polished by forgetting
lies notched with memory, a bloom of rust in the chalk.

A man took it from its dead owner feathered with arrows,
he felt that one's last grip stiffened by mired farmsteads.

It holds the world of burghs as they dissolve; drawn from fire
the sword burns, it has cauterised the world's wound it opened.

The man waves it in the wood, shows the sign of the blade
where the sun levels a blaze like a dead eye in a cold socket.

The warrior leads it home to his hearth, to firelight, torches,
and slowly among his herds and flocks the heat of battle

ebbs out of his brain. The heirloom hangs from a rafter,
its fire out, till death comes with the man's kin to his grave.

They set him on his last journey, the sword he won beside him
and as he dissolves in earth where his bones gleam like chalk

the blade flickers its torchlight to a dull glow of oxides.
Years later it flashes its shape from under the garden,

the slight negative prints of dust man and rust sword
thrust from the garden loam run through with drizzle together.

2

An arm rises from water and catches the falling blade,
the last defence of the land. It is the legend of inheritance,
of benign rule as an enclosure among the ruined villas

built by ghost lords. One morning the pall from their razing
shadows the world's end, till smoke shrinks to its source,
this sword. Burnt vine-rows, blank fields unharvested,

drive a vision of sweet discourse in a well-kept garden
or the sallies of reclining shepherds among the tesserae
to wait in deep woodland a thousand years for Robin,

for the legend of the wooden shaft which pierces steel mail.
Here the invaders puzzle over the ends of cities
emerging from the ground in a theatre of sad farewell,

where the wounded lord calls for his followers and speaks
before they bear him to the pyre. The dead heap up mounds
over their dragon treasures and grave-food for the voyage

laid out beside their swords, as if where swords are planted,
blades will stalwart grow, named like houses or horses,
hilts written with spells. They take leave of the world,

shake off the garment of power regretting they cannot side-step
death's masterful stroke. Yet they take beyond life
their eldest strongest friend to embrace in fellowship for ever.

3

Hammer the blade, then hold the wonder aloft:
red with heat it will be plunged into water,
to seethe and hiss and be edged with herbs of power

while words are woven in its secret ceremony.
Spirits of earth and water churn and change,
but give up strength to blackened steel unhoned,

as the blade-maker raises it, and shouts, and shows it forth
with a sign cut in air. It is naked, and cries out,
it has much to learn from the ignorance of the arm,

from the dumb strength directed by the back, as weight
shifts power to the shoulder and welds sword to hand.
The sword in its wrappings will lie nights in the arms

of the captain restless for battle armed at first light.
Bride blade, best comrade, let the slug-a-bed lie.
The archaeologist's spade taps over him its lullaby.

PATCHES OF PATTERNING

Patches of yellow patterning
on our lawn never greened, even
coaxed with soil and fertiliser:
there was something underneath.
A man who lived here once
bought derelict cars, swapped parts
to build a perfect example,
then disposed of the unused bits
in a deep hole and grassed it over.

I spent painful hours digging,
till I struck metal. I streaked
my arms and face with rust orange,
turned up sections of chassis,
parts of engines, bunched wiring,
perished rubber, empty shapes,
stains in soil, sand in layers:
where real investigators
trowel and brush faint differences

from earth where wood has been,
my effort just raised blisters
and grazed my arms. I sat there
exhausted beside the pile, tipped
water on my head from a bottle
wondering what on earth I'd done.
Answering question marks in grass
solved no murder, found no treasure
but heaped into a burden: now
it would never go under again,

too much would be left over.
The discovery settled and hardened
into a depression. I remembered
as a child scooping a pit
on a sandy beach and the tide
smoothing it over. Impermanence
was a shock then, but now it seems
worse that things don't vanish,
that stubborn traces cover me over
with patches of yellow patterning.

SILENT POOL

A white clay cup, pool in a thicket, suspended
afternoon, no breath of wind or bird call.

A bowl of clear water the day I saw it,
holding still its tale of the drowned maiden

fleeing from the mounted savage lord intent
on ravishment. Hence the hush of the place,

its refuge of deep water without motion,
inhuman element. Here her self dissolved,

sinking below the earth's grasp and possession,
hallowed, unfollowed. We all bow our heads,

then push through undergrowth to reach the road
and cycle against the wind. The cold air

makes her shape, her absence, more definite.

STONE TURTLE

Rising from deepest water, a sculpted stone
afloat in time, it turns and sinks back,

detached from accepted meaning, now upwards,
now downwards, stub neck and ancient head

nudging the polished surface of its display case,
as if in the water cistern packed with rock debris

dug out by East India Company engineers
from the fragments of a ruined paradise,

an absolute statement from the ideal menagerie
their Ruler assembled once. Shrugging off dust

of that solid, dead kingdom, it falls and rises
in the flow of oblivion, a perfect river turtle

honed and agile, and swims confidently on,
a ripple on the gleaming surface of impermanence.

TIME BACKWARDS

1

The typescript of the house deeds turn into calligraphy
the title to the Great Field in the hands of the land agent.

Strips of plough, a fringe of wood, the disputed hedgerows
mapped for enclosure; accustomed days of mattock and plough

given to the manor or taken, and named one way in speech
and another on parchment rolls, decorated with bird hoppings

in snow, black letter, stubble burning, patient field paths:
the king's book's Latin overwriting the thane's thorn's flowering.

2

August's cropmarks wave the imprint of wall and enclosure,
a memory of longboats drives beasts and tribes down;

however deep you dig you'll find no footsteps or cries;
warriors leaning on spear shafts which rooted and grew farmers;

mounds of graves, the endowment, settling with small invaders,
fox and vole, and the axe-blade, the marauder's sound in
woodland;

unsettlement, a smoke-plume blackening tile and flint;
fields for veterans enrolled with the enemy's twisted torc;

far from downland where mammoth slumber in their sediment
with the memory of their strength, the assuredness of possession.

THE ORDINARY

ELY APHRODITE

In the Lady Chapel the statuary has crumbled
but a fat new shiny Madonna has been installed,
empty as the last small Russian doll. The divine

has migrated from the cathedral, across the road
round the corner and through the kind of garden
a goddess might once have sat in. It is tea-time

and the tall young waitress, a local sixth-former
working for pocket-money, brings the tray,
gravely walking and trying hard not to drop it,

her complexion pale rose-petal white and red,
her grace quite innocent, and her kind beauty
shining in a smile as she carefully places on the table

a vase of fresh flowers, cups of tea for us both,
sweet cake white with caster, and asks what else
she can do for us, and pauses shyly for an answer.

THE ORDINARY

Aegean

On that windy island where the dust path led on
through scrub and boulders, low twisted trees
all shaped to lean inland, a long brown snake
lay dead across the way. I cast a stone at it
then edged a detour through the parched shrubs,
drooping dry bushes, cropped shocks of thyme
and sage, then climbed rough-hewn slab steps
around and higher, and out along the cliff-top.

Up there the sea wind bathed my face, I gulped
gratefully cooling air. Further on, the cleft rock
reached above the waves in a long promontory
sloping and sheltered. There at the very edge of it
a man wearing a tall hat sat fishing, his long line
hanging over a deep pool carved by endless waves
cradled by rock walls. In calm air, alone, unmoving
he sat, stared and smoked, just waiting for a bite,

that priest with his Greek beard and black robe.
I waved a greeting, he raised a hand, palm open,
in a muted blessing, or so it seemed. Just fishing,
and not for souls, being blown by the ocean air,
sitting at his ease on the edge of ordinariness
where it touches the matters of the soul, the mystery
of our coming and going, or at least crashes against it
with an eruption of sea spray and splash of noise.

GOAT LAND

Astypalia

In early morning June sun on a dry slope
pigs lie out to warm, the young huddled together
in lines along the hill, their long grey mothers

dusted all over. The bright red-brown shapes
of pacing and pecking hens patrol a field corner
of scrub grass and weed. A few trees lean

beyond the wire fence and this shady enclosure
walled one side with an old bedstead, the other
of whitewashed breezeblocks. In a corner on the floor,

just rutted concrete, lies a black goat, the father
of the place it seems, his rough coat full of twigs,
leaves and dirt, like a god resting after creation.

Here he has taken refuge after his many labours.
When we pass we feed him handfuls of torn weed
and olive tree fronds. Your hand rubs at his nose,

then searches in his tangled fleece and discovers
dried up windfall olives and sprouting seeds. Perhaps
it hides shards of red-painted vases, silver coins,

scroll fragments of holy text. His dark eyes
search in our human ones for midday shade,
for green stalks to chew at, for traces of paths,

but find a dusty blankness, an unkempt world
where ones just like him can be hobbled with a chain
among sun-bathing pigs and hungry pacing hens.

JASMINE

Athens 1977

Heading home up the hill each night
numbed by work, sweaty from the bus,
I step up past neighbourhood flats,
their looming balconied dark shapes
lit with squares of light, alive
with low voices, clattering of plates.

Sounds patter at the pavement trees,
the road leads up to sky, faint shapes
with the roar of jets turning to descend.
All to be learned - city, language,
how quiet spaces numbed by traffic
might yet be planted with cypress and olive,

with an old man reading Mickey Mouse,
and children at play who run and shout.
The place blossoms with the unexpected,
as here this cloud of cheap air freshener
or something like it wafting as I pass,
emerges as the heavy scent of jasmine

sudden in the mind, heavy and new.

FLIP SIDE

The model of the ruined city lies in a polished glass case
faint lines of walls, gouged out rock and earth,
its perimeter the footings of walls felled long ago.

Like the underside of a sea monster's carapace
the hollow of its life and its seething outer skin lie
under, extending down through the floor,

passing by the foundations of this extensive building
and shading the rock below with its brooding life,
settled unmoving like a huge stone, waiting for its prey,

lapped by the all involving ocean which contains
everything there has ever been, and the ruin
of whatever is left to come. We stare down at the glass,

past our faces reflected in its sheen, at the flip side
of streets which once ran with shouts, with smoke
writhing its welcome from neighbouring houses

and find ourselves staring into two half-lidded eyes,
liquid depths poised just above the water line
their inner inhuman vacancy preparing to be filled.

BROADCAST

Astipalia

We saw her on the TV
as we sat in the house at coffee
– reception was none too good –
but there was the old woman
her grey head scarf-bound
needles busy in gnarled hands –
shepherds gave her the wool
which she carded and spun.

The island was almost empty
few autumn tourists lingering.
We'd walk to beaches and back,
up to the castle in the heat
and later, when shadows cooled,
sat and ate. That was time
for a stroll in the narrow streets,
past ruins occupied by cats.

There by light of a street lamp
she sat knitting and waiting,
for us it seemed. We asked
about her work – goat wool socks –
and then paid far too much.
Her lined face and her shape
showed hard years, little to remain,
a few dead leaves broadcast
on an island bowed by the wind.

SUMMER

Attiki

Small islands near to shore, Helen, Patroclus
A stray dog eyes the shadow of the marathon runner
The eucalyptus uncurls a little more papyrus

Evening limps downhill with poor pierced ankles
The giantess leaps from the cinema into my room
A battered helmet turns again in the river shallows

Now an arrow-head flakes from memory's obsidian
An island shifts and snores and scratches at a shoulder
And the pulsing of the sun begins, the pulsing of the sun

Notes

Camberwell: people in this section either lived in Camberwell, or had a connection with the area. Others mentioned e.g. John Perceval, have relevance to the subject of the poem.

p.1   *the Tower at Elephant*: a building at Elephant and Castle.

p.3   *Eleanor Coade*: proprietor 1770s to 1820s of the Coade works at Lambeth, which produced statues, columns, and other architectural items, cast in moulds from an artificial stone, a very durable ceramic. Hundreds of these works still exist. See Alison Kelly: *Mrs Coade's Stone*.

p.4   *Lava Rink*: roller skating rink opened in 1876, first home of roller hockey, 1885.

p.4   *James Plimpton*: patented first modern roller skates in the USA in 1863. The paired wheels could move slightly as the skater leaned left or right, rather than being fixed rigidly to the base of the skate, as in earlier skates.

p.7   *Free House*: the two quotations are from David Copperfield.

p.10   *John Coakley Lettsom*: *Family Portrait* in the Wellcome Collection, London. For Lettsom, see James Johnston Abraham: *Lettsom*.

p.15   *John Ruskin*: Art critic and social critic, 1819-1900, whose ideas influenced (and still influence) many artists, social reformers, politicians, town planners, and environmentalists, among others.

p.15   *The Passenger Pigeon*: N. American pigeon once abundant, but hunted to extinction by the early 20th century.

p.16   *Mary Ann Girling*: see Philip Hoare: *England's Lost Eden*.

p.21   *John Perceval (1803-1876)*: son of assassinated British Prime Minister Spencer Perceval. Wrote an account of his own mental breakdown, *Perceval's Narrative*. Later campaigned for the rights of the mentally ill. See Sarah Wise: *Inconvenient People*.

p.40   *House on the Shore*: partly a translation, partly a recasting of Montale's poem.

p.41   *A Voyage to Kythera*: Baudelaire's poem sees only death, horror and disgust in what is a reaction to an earlier French tradition in which Kythera or Cythera, one of the birthplaces of Aphrodite, is an imagined paradise peopled by happy lovers, as in the painting by Watteau. These are both versions of myth or psychology, rather than visits to the real island.

p.47   *Eltham*: site of a medieval palace in SE London, with a 15th century Great Hall, and an art Deco house of 1933 occupying the old palace site.

p.48   *Adam of Usk*: Welsh cleric present at the visit of the Emperor. He wrote a chronicle of his life and times.

p.52   The poem evokes the theme of 17th century 'country house' poems. Notable examples are by Emilia Lanier, Ben Jonson, Thomas Carew and Andrew Marvell. The quotation is from Virginia Woolf's *Diaries*.

www.ingramcontent.com/pod-product-compliance
Lightning Source LLC
Chambersburg PA
CBHW021158080526
44588CB00008B/398